GW00671135

Margaret Clitherow

by
Jean Olwen Maynard

*All booklets are published thanks to the
generous support of the members of the
Catholic Truth Society*

CATHOLIC TRUTH SOCIETY
PUBLISHERS TO THE HOLY SEE

CONTENTS

Margaret Clitherow

Beginnings

Following demurely behind her mother, and secretly hugging to herself the thought of how attractive she looked in her best clothes, Margaret tripped round the corner from her home in Davygate, along Coney Street, and into St Martin's Church. As soon as her eyes had adjusted from the glittery winter sunlight outside to the dimness of the interior, she took stock of the changed aspect of the chancel end. Yes, the rood loft was gone. She had known it would be, but it always felt strange to come in to the church and for the first time see something new, or not see something that had been there as far back as she could personally remember.

She could dimly recall, from when she was a small girl, the time that the altars disappeared, and after them the brightly coloured and gilded statues of the saints. The walls were now covered in white plaster, completely plain except for some places where lines of black writing had been inscribed on the plaster. Margaret knew those inscriptions were texts from the Holy Bible, though she had no idea what they said because she'd never been taught to read. She also knew that the rood which had just vanished had not been particularly old. The huge crucifix, together with its companion statues of Our Lady and St John, was completed and erected into place in 1555, when her father Thomas Middleton was one of the church wardens. That was fifteen years ago, when Margaret herself was about two, so of course she couldn't actually remember it happening. However she'd heard her father talk about it.

During the last few years of his life, Thomas Middleton was very ill and bedridden, and in considerable pain from his gout, so his immediate family had had to listen to a fair amount of grumbling. One of his pet moans was about the parish having constantly to fork out money because of the see-sawing of the government's religious policy: first smash the furnishings, then order expensive replacements, then smash the new ones, and so it went on. A lot of the work done on the church during his churchwardenship had been undone just a few years later. Since he was a candlemaker by trade, the prohibition on lighting candles for devotional purposes had also hurt his business. The waste of money and loss of trade were points to which he repeatedly drew aggrieved attention, but perhaps he did that only to hide deeper feelings which he could not bring himself to articulate, for like most of the citizens of York his heart was with the old ways. However, none of those matters need concern him any longer, for on 16th May 1567 he had been laid in his grave in the centre aisle of the church. Since the law wouldn't allow him to arrange for Masses to be said, he had left small amounts of money to his servants and to the poor of the city, asking simply that they pray for him. Four months later his widow Jane married again, and now in January 1570 the rood loft which he had replaced in compliance with the directives of Queen Mary had, in compliance with the directives of Queen Elizabeth, been torn down by Henry May - Jane's new husband, and Margaret's stepfather.

Henry May - an ambitious man

Originally from Hampshire, Henry May had arrived in York with no money and no connections. Ordinarily he would have had no chance of securing an apprenticeship, and so working his way up to guild membership and the right to establish his own shop or business. Since too many masters in any one trade would mean none of them could make a decent living, the guilds strictly limited the number of apprentices any member could take on. But for over a century the once-great northern city had been in economic decline, because its traditional cloth industry could no longer compete with newly-industrialising small towns and villages where labour costs were cheaper. With the population dropping, and houses falling empty and crumbling into ruin, the Corporation had overruled the guilds to offer easy and attractive terms to draw in newcomers of the right sort. However it was just around the time young Henry arrived in York that its long decline began to be reversed. Queen Elizabeth decreed in 1561 that two important regional government bodies should have their permanent headquarters there: the Council of the North, and the newly-created Ecclesiastical Commission for the Northern Province. Their presence in York represented a great deal of power, power spelled wealth, and wealth spelled conspicuous consumption of goods and services, and plenty of money to be made by providing them. Henry May indentured himself to a vintner to be trained in the relatively new, but rapidly expanding trade in imported wines.

Winning the hand of Jane Middleton gave him a crucial leg-up, for Thomas had left her very well provided for. A particular asset was her large house in Davygate, which the couple quickly turned into a successful inn. The number of inns in York was shooting up, to accommodate all the people coming to bring lawsuits before the Council, and since Jane's father had been an innkeeper she slipped easily and happily into a line of work with which she had been familiar in her younger days. She calmly accepted that Henry had married her for her money. She was in her early fifties, while Henry was considerably younger, yet by the hard-headed standards of the period the match was eminently suitable, for if Jane brought her property and her expertise in keeping the customers happy, Henry brought an unusual cleverness and tremendous charm. This charm he put to work so astutely that, less than a year after his marriage, he had won sufficient social acceptability to be elected one of the city's eight chamberlains or treasurers. Civic office was prestigious but unpaid, and could entail considerable expense; nevertheless, as a clear sign that he had arrived, and was considered solid and reliable, it was an excellent way for Henry to improve his longer-term opportunities for increasing his wealth, as well as his status and political influence.

Service as one of the churchwardens of St Martin's also advanced his personal ambitions. York's new Archbishop, Edmund Grindal, was determined to enforce the government's latest round of directives concerning public worship. Henry May not only showed himself zealous in implementing the directives, but claimed to approve of them with all his heart. Sure enough, less than a year after he tore down the St Martin's rood screen, he was sworn in as sheriff, a post which involved particularly heavy responsibilities in connection with the city's criminal justice system - arresting and holding prisoners, empanelling juries and attending executions. His year in office would make Henry a member of the Corporation, and entitle him to hope one day to be chosen as an alderman - perhaps even Lord Mayor!

Marriage

Margaret's elder sister Alice had been married off long before Henry May appeared on the scene, and her brothers Thomas and George were apprenticed out. But young

Margaret was still at home and, when she turned 18, it was her stepfather who selected a husband for her. John Clitherow was a wealthy sheep-farmer and wholesale dealer in livestock, and also a retail butcher. He was considerably older than Margaret, and had been married before, but his first wife Matilda had died leaving him with two small boys on his hands, and now after a decent period of mourning he was ready to give them a new mother. For a young girl to be matched with a middle-aged widower was not at all unusual, and Margaret went along happily with the arrangement. The wedding was solemnised in St Martin's on 1st July 1571, and once all the feasting was done John could take his beautiful young bride by the arm and walk her triumphantly off - accompanied by an honour guard of boisterous revellers - to his own house just a few streets away in the Shambles.

Once through the front door, Margaret acquired an instant family: William, who was three, and Thomas who was hardly more than a baby. But her new household, like the one over which her mother presided, also included all the servants and apprentices who lived on the premises - most of them even younger than she was herself. Many families could not afford to feed all their children properly, so it was normal practice to hand over growing boys and girls to be brought up by other people, working for their keep but living in far better conditions than they could have expected at home, and often also enjoying a lot of fun together with others of their own age. There was no yawning social chasm between employers and servants, and it was no disgrace for girls of Margaret's own class to go into service. To get a clear picture of Margaret Clitherow's role in life as a married woman, we need to understand the extent to which her "family" included a never-ending stream of other people's pre-teen and adolescent children.

Shop manageress

The wholesale side of John's business took him away from home a lot. Besides the house in the Shambles, which was rented, John had inherited from his father the lease of an estate at Cornbrough, in the parish of Sheriff Hutton about ten miles outside the city. He used the land for pasturing large flocks of sheep but, although the estate included a large house, he rarely slept there overnight. Much more of his time was spent travelling farther afield round rural Yorkshire, making deals over livestock. In his absence Margaret was to manage the shop. This occupied the ground floor front room of the house, the window shutters of which were let down each morning to form a counter. All York's butchers - and there must have been over sixty of them in Margaret's time - lived in the Shambles. They weren't allowed to settle anywhere else, because their work was smelly and extremely messy. "Shambles" literally meant "butcher's stalls", but has come to mean a slaughterhouse or a chaotic mess. In an age without refrigeration or motor transport, the meat for the city's dinners had to be brought in each day to the Shambles on the hoof, and killed and cut up on the spot. That was something else Margaret would have to get used to.

From the start she settled happily into married life. She hadn't married John because she had previously "fallen in love" with him, but their marriage worked. John was delighted to find Margaret trustworthy and capable both as a business partner and a homemaker, and her cheerful welcoming smile was something he could look forward to as he rode wearily into York at the end of his business trips. Margaret found John to be a good provider, who made her a very generous allowance which she was free to spend entirely as she wished on fine clothes and trinkets; he also respected her abilities and left her free in her own sphere of action. Of course she had to work hard and shoulder a lot of responsibility, but the nature of her work was largely managerial; she wasn't expected to do the more boring, or messy and distasteful, tasks herself. Juggling family responsibilities and a business career was relatively unstressful because her world was so conveniently arranged: her home was also her workplace, and she always had other people around to help with childcare or minding the shop. Shopping requirements and social engagements took her from time to time into other parts of the city, but for most purposes she didn't have far to go. If she walked south along the Shambles and turned the corner, she found herself in the Pavement, where a market was held three times a week. Walking north to the top of the street brought her to her new parish church of Holy Trinity, King's Court, popularly known as Christ Church. It was Christ Church which she now attended with John each Sunday, and where her first child was brought for baptism - a son who was given the name Henry, after his godfather Henry May.

Banquets

During their first few years together, the newlyweds' interests meshed well, and they led a very active social life. Social occasions were never completely separate from business concerns, because success in the Elizabethan world was very dependent on keeping in with the right people. But for those who were doing well in life and ambitious to do better still, this only added to the attraction. Both John and Margaret took great delight in accepting invitations to banquets where they would enjoy good food, in good and potentially useful company. Often these banquets were organised by the butchers at their guildhall, paid for by participants at so much a head, except when a deceased tradesman left money in his will for his colleagues to enjoy a meal in his memory. The Clitherows also received frequent invitations to social gatherings - especially weddings - from relatives, friends and business acquaintances. Many invitations came from rural areas well outside the city; because John was so often away, it was quite common for Margaret to go without him, riding in company with a group of neighbours who had also been invited. But the couple did like to go to banquets together, whenever they could. When, a few years later, Margaret began to reorder her priorities in life, her interests would change quite radically, but by then she and John had already built up a solid, loving relationship.

Unwillingly Protestant

It used to be generally believed that the Protestant Reformation in this country came about in response to popular demand. The vast majority of the population were supposed to have been alienated by the "meaningless ceremonies" of the Mediaeval Church, and disgusted at the corruption and greed of the clergy, and so responded to the advent of Protestantism with warm enthusiasm. Historians now acknowledge that the evidence does not bear it out, and that if the English had been given a genuinely free choice, they would have opted to stay Catholic. But if the religious changes were so widely disliked, why did people put up with them without protest? The answer is simple: they *had* protested. In 1536 York welcomed the Pilgrimage of Grace, an armed mass demonstration ostensibly aimed at ridding King Henry

VIII of the "evil councillors" who had led him astray. The King's agents met the Pilgrims with fair words and promises that their grievances would be listened to, so persuading them to disperse; soon afterwards their leaders were rounded up and put to death. York got off relatively lightly, in exchange for a humble public apology and over a thousand pounds in "gifts" and "benevolences" to the King and Queen Katherine Howard. The citizens had learned their lesson: protest, it seemed, was useless, so they must learn to live with the situation.

The Elizabethan religious settlement was imposed from the top down, and deliberately designed as a compromise, so it's not surprising that most people found it neither convincing nor inspiring. The spiritual cutting edge of the English Reformation was represented by the Puritans, whose understanding of Christianity was framed on the theological teachings of John Calvin; but Puritanism, as we know, never became widely popular in England as it did in Scotland. Most people in York dutifully turned up to the compulsory Sunday services in their parish church, and did not complain too openly. Gradually a few of them emerged as sincere converts to the "Reformed" approach to Christianity, while others - like Henry May - were at least keen to put on a show of solid Protestantism in order to advance both their personal interests and those of the community. But a very high proportion continued to "mislike" the public services. Substantial numbers were "church papists" who only attended to avoid trouble; in their hearts they regarded themselves as Catholics, and they would hear Mass in secret when they thought it safe to do so. A tiny minority of recusants, by flatly refusing to be present at Protestant services and being prepared to risk a great deal to hear Mass, made themselves liable to criminal penalties. Already at the time of Margaret's marriage a small number of recusant Catholics - both priests and laypeople - were languishing in prison in York Castle.

The Catholic Earl of Northumberland

In 1572 the Pavement in York was chosen as the scene for the public execution of Thomas Percy, Earl of Northumberland. Earl Thomas, a genial aristocrat beloved of his own tenantry, and generally popular throughout the north, had been one of the leaders of the Northern Rebellion of 1569, which raised again the banner of the Pilgrimage of Grace and had among its aims the restoration "of the old and Catholic religion". On its failure he escaped to Scotland, but was treacherously handed over by the Scottish government in exchange for a money payment of £2,000. Having got him, the English government first sentenced him to be beheaded, and then offered him his life if he would renounce his Catholic faith. To induce such a prominent Catholic leader to conform to the state church would have been a major coup, but the Earl turned down the offer, and the fact that he did so gave his impending death an entirely different meaning: he would die a Catholic martyr. During his last night in York Castle, he was not allowed to see any of the priests being held there, but when he was led out the following day, it was insisted that William Palmer, the Protestant Chancellor of York Minster, accompany him to the scaffold. Palmer was to try for a last-minute conversion, in order to snatch a propaganda success out of an affair that was turning out all wrong. Margaret at the time must either have been heavily pregnant, or nursing baby Henry, and probably wasn't actually present, but she must have been very aware of what was going on, and would have heard the whole story afterwards.

As the Earl mounted onto the platform, Palmer began pestering him to make a speech to the crowd acknowledging himself a traitor to the Queen, and as such justly condemned. "At this the Earl, turning towards the people, said, 'I should have been content to meet my death in silence, were it not that I see it is the custom for those who undergo this kind of punishment to address some words to the bystanders as to the cause of their being put to death. Know, therefore, that from my earliest years down to this present day, I have held the Faith of that Church which, throughout the whole Christian world, is knit and bound together; and in that same Faith I am about to end this unhappy life. But as for this new English church, I do not acknowledge it.' Here Palmer, interrupting him, cried out in a loud voice; 'I see that you are dying an obstinate Papist; a member, not of the Catholic, but of the Roman Church.' To this the Earl replied: 'That which you call the Roman Church is the Catholic Church, which has been founded on the teaching of the Apostles, Jesus Christ himself being its corner-stone, strengthened by the blood of Martyrs, honoured by the recognition of the holy Fathers; and it continues always the same, being the Church against which, as Christ our Saviour said, the gates of Hell shall not prevail.'" Adding that "if he had a thousand lives he would give them up for the Catholic faith," he "begged all present to forgive him, declaring that he on his part forgave all from his heart," then folded his arms over his breast in the form of a cross and stretched himself on the block. As his head was struck off the spectators "called on God to receive his soul into eternal rest" and rushed forward to dip their handkerchiefs into his blood to be preserved as relics of the martyr. Earl Percy's severed head was displayed on a pole over Micklegate Bar, but his body was buried in the Church of Holy Cross at the corner of the Shambles and the Pavement.

The Protestant Earl of Huntingdon

On 29th November 1572 Queen Elizabeth's kinsman Henry Hastings, Earl of Huntingdon, arrived in York to take over as the new Lord President of her Council in the North. A deeply sincere and zealous Protestant of the dynamic Puritan school, he was determined to back up Archbishop Grindal's campaign to stamp out the "old superstitions". Pressure must be brought to bear at all levels, including the parishes which were the smallest units of both ecclesiastical and civil government. A few days before Christmas, John Clitherow and some of his neighbours were called to a meeting at Christ Church and informed that they had been selected, as "discreet and honest" parishioners, to assist the churchwardens and parish constables in implementing the High Commission's zero tolerance line. Their job would be "to enquire and truly without favour or affection certify the names and dwelling places of all known or suspected Papists within your rule and charge, the enemies of God and good order, and namely of such that do not come to the church to hear divine service and sermons according to the laws of God and the common order now established by the laws of this realm."

The discreet and honest parishioners found themselves in a painful dilemma. One of the churchwardens, William Hutton, was thoroughly Catholic in outlook and soon to become a recusant himself. But whatever their personal beliefs, none of them wanted to have to shop any of their friends, neighbours or relatives to the authorities. Dissidents were regarded sometimes with irritation, but usually at the same time also with considerable sympathy, and in the last resort genuine respect. Among the Christ Church parishioners was Dr Thomas Vavasour, a Cambridge graduate well able to argue in defence of his Catholic faith. So notorious was he for his opposition to Queen Elizabeth's religious settlement that he had been publicly excommunicated in York Minster, and gone into hiding. Government agents had been hunting for him already for four years, without success. The best the churchwardens could do to shield him was to declare that they had no idea where he was, and quite probably they were telling the truth - though quite probably they had been scrupulously careful not to find out. In his absence his wife Dorothy was performing a valued service in the locality, by offering board and lodging to women during childbirth. Although women always gave birth "at home", there was a distinct advantage if it could be a home other than their own, somewhere where there could be no question of their having to struggle out of bed too soon after delivery to deal with a domestic crisis; the convenience of such an arrangement was also welcomed by many husbands. At Mrs Vavasour's it was rumoured that, for those who wished for it, spiritual counsel and sacramental ministrations were also available, from godly priests of the old kind. Childbirth was a dangerous time, and if anything did go wrong ... well, most of them, in their heart of hearts, would feel easier to think that a priest could be at hand.

Margaret's conversion

The courageous death of Earl Thomas had made a strong impression on Margaret Clitherow, and over the intervening years she had been doing some thinking. The availability of properly trained Protestant clergy at that date was necessarily limited, and it was limited still further by the fact that some of the most enthusiastic Puritans were too extreme, or simply too eccentric, to be acceptable to the state church. However Lord Huntingdon was notoriously willing to protect such enthusiasts, and both he and Archbishop Grindal were very keen to deploy them as preachers in the north of England. They ensured that in York, at least, the Protestant message was excellently well presented, in its most logical and persuasive form. Not every parish could be allocated a top quality preacher, but several were kept on the staff at York Minster: William Palmer was one, and another was Edmund Bunney. Everyone was encouraged to attend their special sermons at the Minster. Going by the quiet confidence that Margaret was to show later on when confronted with the cream of the local Protestant clergy, she must already have heard the best possible explanations of their theology, thought hard about it, and arrived at her own conclusion - which was that she could find "no substance, truth nor Christian comfort in the ministers of the new gospel, nor in their doctrine itself".

During her second pregnancy, Margaret was a frequent visitor at Dorothy Vavasour's home. Possibly she began going even earlier, to see friends or neighbours who were staying there. She had an ideal excuse, for it was normal at childbirth for any number of "gossips" (women friends) to be called round, as much for moral support as for experienced assistance, and to refuse would have been unneighbourly. Since she can't have been under any illusions about the ethos of the Vavasour household, it's likely that she was deliberately seeking a clearer idea of what the Catholic faith was about. She must already have known many of the basic Christian teachings which had been taken over unchallenged by Protestantism, and been familiar with the key stories in the Old Testament and the Gospels - perhaps from hearing them read aloud in church, but more likely from seeing them vividly enacted in the streets of York by the trade guilds, which continued to stage the traditional Mystery Plays up to 1570. Her problem was how to place all those jigsaw pieces into a coherent framework, since the one offered by Protestantism didn't satisfy her. Despite the persistence all around her of pre-Reformation customs and scraps of wisdom, she was quite hazy about how the Catholic belief system fitted together.

Of the Catholic priests ordained under Queen Mary, a significant number had come to the decision not to continue working in the government-controlled church;

they had resigned their posts and disappeared, and were now travelling around conducting a clandestine ministry. Dorothy Vavasour arranged for her to speak to one of these priests, his explanations made sense to her, and everything fell into place. At some point late in 1573 or early in 1574, Margaret was reconciled to the Catholic Church. Her daughter Anne, born in 1574 probably just after Margaret's conversion, may have been taken for baptism at Christ Church, but Margaret herself no longer attended Anglican services.

Recusancy

From this time on she faced the problem (common to most married women through the ages!) that to gain a few hours of real privacy she had to resort to subterfuge. It wasn't that John was spying on her or keeping her shut up in the house - and in any case he wasn't there a lot of the time. But she was the focal point around which the household revolved, and she couldn't just disappear without giving a plausible reason. To state openly that she was engaged in something illegal would put her husband embarrassingly on the spot. Besides, most of her staff, let alone her children, were very young and might innocently blurt out the dangerous truth to the wrong people - and if she was unconcerned about the risks to herself personally, she had to consider the safety of others. One solution was obvious: she continued to be readily available whenever called on to help out with a lying-in at Mrs Vavasour's, and it wasn't difficult to arrange for a fake summons suitably timed to enable her to keep appointments with her confessor, or attend Mass.

Another ploy to which Margaret resorted is more difficult to make sense of. It was described years later by her first biographer, a priest named Fr Mush, but either he himself didn't quite understand how she'd worked it, and hadn't bothered to ask, or else the details were so obvious that it never occurred to him to spell them out. When the newly-Catholic Margaret set off with her neighbours for a country wedding, she would ride with them out of the city as before but, about a mile along the route, someone would be waiting by prior arrangement and they would swap places, allowing Margaret to slip away for a meeting with her spiritual adviser. It's a puzzle to see how such an impersonation could have been worked. Could the new fashion of women wearing masks at social gatherings have had something to do with it? Possibly some of these wedding invitations came from livestock farmers who knew John Clitherow well, but had never met his wife, or possibly the invitation was so loose that a kinswoman of Margaret's would happily have been welcomed in her stead. But if she was travelling with a group of people who knew her reasonably well, they at least must have been aware of the changeover, and prepared to collude with the subterfuge.

Margaret's conversion was never a strict personal or family secret. She always had to be careful, especially with people she didn't know well, for if she behaved suspiciously or spoke indiscreetly in front of a stranger who turned out to be a zealous Protestant, she might find herself in serious trouble. But most of her neighbours and acquaintances could be trusted. Whenever she nipped round for a gossip, and especially when they were all chatting happily together at banquets and other social gatherings, she talked eagerly to them about her new-found faith. As Fr Mush put it, "She had a vehement desire that all others, both heretics, schismatics, and lukewarm Catholics, might know God and his truth, be made children of his Catholic Church, serve and love him above all things, and obtain no less grace than she wished for herself; that God might be glorified in all his people."

Fr Mush's account had to be scrupulously careful in most instances never to mention names, but the growing circle of recusants in Christ Church parish is known to have included Janet, wife of Percival Geldard, and Anne who was married to John Clitherow's cousin John Weddell. Both their husbands, like Margaret's, were wealthy butchers. However Margaret's support network of sympathisers and collaborators was by no means confined to fellow-recusants. Because butchers' families tended to intermarry, ties of kinship linked many of the households in the Shambles, making the street a very close-knit community. For example, the families who lived (and kept butcher's shops) in the houses adjoining the Clitherow's were both related to John: on one side lived William Calvert, married to John's sister Millicent; and on the other Michael and Ellen Mudd who were related to John's first wife. Over and above ties of blood or friendship, many of Margaret's publicly conformist neighbours still saw themselves as Catholics. Margaret, as one committed to strict compliance with the Church's requirements, believed their attendance at state church services to be a deadly sin, and up to a point this must have annoyed them. But she obviously didn't come across to them as judgmental or holier-than-thou, and there's no evidence that her stance made her generally unpopular. People who are not living up to what they truly believe are often strongly attracted to someone who is, and who will straightforwardly point out to them the implications of their lack of integrity, even if they have no intention of changing their lifestyle ... or at least, not yet. It's likely too that Margaret benefited from an instinctive solidarity among women, closing ranks to protect their homely, people-centred world from the confusing demands of the outside world. In rallying round to safeguard each other, the housewives tacitly enlisted as allies their children and servants rather than their fathers and husbands, those adult male heads of families who, whatever else, had to deal with that outside world, and who were better off not knowing too much.

Arrests and imprisonments

Even Dorothy Vavasour's nerves proved unable to cope with a ferocious raid on her house which took place in 1574, when the Council of the North was tipped off that Dr Vavasour was making a secret visit to his family. Lord Huntingdon's retainers spent all day searching the place, breaking down walls and ripping up floorboards, yet the Vavasours' special hiding place was so carefully constructed that they didn't find it. Eventually they gave up searching, but ordered the Mayor to post armed watchmen in the house to starve Dr Vavasour out. The watchers stayed all night and all through the following day before he gave himself up. He could have held out for longer, but there was a priest hiding with him: once the doctor surrendered the watch was called off, and the priest was able to escape. So afraid were the authorities of Dr Vavasour that instead of imprisoning him in York, where he might talk to and influence his fellow-prisoners, they resolved to send him "to a solitary prison in the queen's majesty's castle at Hull where he shall only talk to walls." Dorothy suffered a breakdown during the raid, but soon made a full recovery. Her house continued to serve as the city's main Mass centre, and a welcoming refuge for hunted Catholics.

Archbishop Grindal was replaced in 1575 but his successor, Edwin Sandys, continued his policies. Janet Geldard was summoned before the High Commission to explain her persistent absence from Sunday services;

when, rather than offering humble excuses, she stated firmly that her refusal to attend was a matter of principle, she was imprisoned in York Castle. The High Commission then increased the pressure on the Corporation, who in turn put pressure on the churchwardens of each parish to report their absentees. In June, reluctantly, Christ Church produced a list: Janet Geldard was on it, as were Dorothy Vavasour and Anne Weddell, and also "the wife of John Clitherow". The list for November again mentioned Margaret Clitherow who "cometh not to the church, for what cause we cannot learn, for she is now great with child, and could not come before us."

Margaret continued to run up a long backlog of fines for missing church until the summer of 1577, when the High Commission resolved to crack down on the resurgent Catholicism among the city's leading women. They started with Lady Dineley: her husband John, Lord Mayor of York, was treated to a lecture along the lines of "a man who is set to govern a city and cannot govern his own household", and fined 40s. Alderman Robert Cripling, and another member of the Corporation named George Hall who was a prominent draper in Christ Church parish, also had recusant wives. Hall claimed to have "now and then beaten" his over the issue; if he was telling the truth, it had clearly failed to bring her to a more Protestant frame of mind. On 2nd August John and Margaret Clitherow were called before the High

Commissioners, together with several other couples. John assured them that he would do everything he could to advise his wife to attend in future (he couldn't promise that she actually would) but he refused to pay the fines. The other husbands said the same as John. All of them were sent to the Kidcote, one of a group of small municipal prisons on Ouse Bridge, while Margaret and the other wives were locked up in the Castle. After three days, thanks to the Archbishop's intervention, the husbands were released - but not their recusant womenfolk.

York Castle

The Castle was the county gaol for Yorkshire, but it wasn't particularly fearsome. A collection of ramshackle old houses stood within the crumbling courtyard walls; these had been joined together by makeshift knock-throughs and passageways and - except for a few unfortunates who, as a punishment or for security reasons, were locked up in underground dungeons - prisoners were simply assigned rooms in them. Like all Elizabethan prisons, the Castle was contracted out to private management, and the prisoners had to pay for meals, heating and laundry. The gaolers also offered all sorts of "privileges" in return for a suitable consideration, so that prison life could be reasonably comfortable for those who had money available - though even so it was notoriously unhealthy, and liable to shorten their life expectancy if unduly prolonged. John presumably did his best to ensure that Margaret had all she needed. Nevertheless, the whole pattern of her life changed abruptly, in ways that were potentially very depressing. She was separated from her children: her two young stepsons William and Thomas, Henry and Anne who were five and three respectively, and presumably the baby she was carrying the previous winter. Just because Elizabethan mothers were so strict with their children, and never talked much about their feelings for them, there's no reason to think they didn't care. She was also separated from her husband for a much longer period than any of his business trips, since it was over three months before John was allowed to visit her. Finally, for the first time in her life she had no practical work to occupy her time and energies.

Looking on the bright side, however, she had several close friends in prison with her, including Janet Geldard and Anne Weddell, and the married couple Edward and Anne Tesh. Careful not to let anyone sit around getting depressed, the imprisoned Catholics developed a structured community life with sharing of material resources, group prayer and discussion, in order to provide mutual support. No one must be allowed to brood in solitude. Nor must people be allowed to fall into an attitude of stoical resignation, gritting their teeth to keep going in the face of a suffering perceived as not only undeserved but pointless. The ways of God's providence were a deep mystery, but their faith called them to see the disaster that had fallen on their Church, and on them personally, as being ordered to a good purpose. A popular approach was to interpret their sufferings as a way of making reparation for the sins of the Church in former generations. Since some prisoners had sufficient food and some very little, they pooled what they did have and - because it was barely enough to go round - agreed that everyone would observe four days in each week as fast-days. So on Monday, Wednesday, Friday and Saturday nobody ate meat, and they all made do with just one very simple meal. In this way a hardship was given a meaning and turned into a blessing.

William Palmer and Edmund Bunney were supposed to come once a month to carry out an inspection, and check that the regulations drawn up for the supervision of the imprisoned Catholics were being strictly observed. Nevertheless the regulations were not strictly observed, since bribes for turning a blind eye were a major source of income for the gaolers. Because the prison buildings were a complete labyrinth, devotional articles and liturgical equipment could easily be kept hidden, and when, as quite often happened, a priest happened to be among the prisoners, confession and Mass were available far more easily than on the outside. Bunney assembled them from time to time for friendly little talks, to try to persuade them of the errors of their ways, and they were forced to listen - though they did have some scope for answering back. His pet line was to play everyone along by expressing warm agreement with Catholic ideas, and then go on to argue that any differences with Protestantism were really too trivial to make a fuss about. After he had gone, they got together for a thorough discussion, to help resolve any confusion he might have raised in anyone's mind. From time to time news filtered through to them of further arrests, and whenever a new prisoner was brought in they all crowded to the window to see. They heard that Anne Foster and her daughters, who "with Mrs Clitherow and others their companions had already with their meetings and assemblies, and even at their gossiping and feasting done much hurt in York, and would do more if they were permitted" had been imprisoned on Ouse Bridge.

Several times over the following winter John and the other husbands were called again before the High Commission, while the authorities struggled to find a solution to the impasse. On 18th November they were given permission to visit their wives, perhaps in the hope that they could persuade them to give in. John found Margaret sharing a room with Anne Weddell, Isabel Porter and Margaret Tailor. Janet Geldard had been ordered to be kept in a separate room on her own - perhaps because she was considered particularly dangerous - but in February all five women were released on bail posted by their husbands. The husbands would be held responsible for ensuring that they did not hold meetings with "disobedient persons", and that they remained essentially under house arrest. In principle they were allowed to leave their houses to go to church, but this of course they were not prepared to do, and for every Sunday and holy day on which they failed to appear at the Protestant service, their husbands had to pay two shillings.

The secret room

Thereafter, on appointed dates twice or three times each year, John Clitherow appeared before the High Commission to post another bond for Margaret and pay her accumulated fines. Whether or not he knew it, she had no intention whatsoever of complying with the restrictions imposed on her. Their neighbours on either side, the Calverts and the Mudds, became recusants under her influence, and she was also busy turning their own house into a Mass centre. Priests left over from the previous reign were getting quite old now, but new ones were being trained at the English College set up across the Channel in Douai by William Allen, and once ordained they slipped quietly back into England and got in touch with the Catholic networks here. In the absence of any proper system of organisation their distribution was partly a matter of chance, but usually two or three were in the York area at any one time. Margaret therefore constructed a secret room where they could stay and celebrate Mass, and where vestments, altar vessels and linen could be stored. The entrance to this room was high up near the roof and very carefully concealed, and the physical space it occupied was in the house of one of her next-door neighbours - so there was no obvious alteration in the layout of the Clitherow house to excite John's suspicions. The door into it was very narrow, and difficult to negotiate unless you knew the trick of it. Margaret was no longer interested in personal adornment or trivial luxuries, so she could devote all the generous allowance which John still gave her to her religious activities; the room was therefore very well-equipped, but inside it was a concealed hiding place in which to store the Catholic books, vestments and altar vessels, so that it could quickly be made to look completely innocent. Finally the room had an emergency exit, to enable anyone in it to escape by a back way if Margaret's house were raided.

As a result of her prison experience, Margaret's life-style changed in many ways besides losing interest in fine clothes and jewellery. She had developed a taste for quiet and prayer, and she kept up the abstemious eating habits she had got used to, with frequent fasting and a preference for rye bread and butter, milk, and pottage (a nourishing vegetable soup thickened with oats or barley). Pottage was what most poor people made do with every day, and it sounds quite healthy. But for anyone able to afford the large quantities of meat which well-off people normally enjoyed - and Margaret was a butcher's wife! - it was amazingly abstemious. She no longer enjoyed the banquets she used to love so much, because it was impossible to go to them and not over-indulge. Poor John! He had already been put to considerable inconvenience, loss of time and money for the sake of her religious commitment - which he never shared - and it must have been a heavy blow for him to find that she didn't want to go out with him any more to parties. He didn't like it, but he put up with it: she was his wife, and he loved her. Another change, which John probably never noticed, was that Margaret began taking on herself quite a lot of rather messy, boring or unpleasant little household tasks like making up the fires, sweeping the floor, washing up dishes or emptying chamber pots. Although she had never been a "lady of leisure", she had always been able to leave tasks of this kind to the servants, but while in prison she had had to muck in and do her share, and now she kept up the habit.

A subversive corpse

On the Feast of the Assumption, 15th August 1578, the city sheriffs burst into Dorothy Vavasour's house while the feastday Mass was being celebrated. The priest and several lay Catholics were arrested. Mrs Vavasour later appeared before Archbishop Sandys (and wouldn't give him an inch) but - amazingly - even at this juncture her social connections managed to save her from gaol. Meanwhile, still in prison on the Ouse Bridge, Anne Foster fell ill and died. The minister from nearby St John's Church, who came to arrange for the funeral, found the dead woman holding in her hand a profession of faith, a demand for Catholic burial, and an explicit rejection of his services. By this act Anne succeeded posthumously in setting the whole city in an uproar. The minister had her body brought out and laid publicly on the bridge, whereupon a crowd collected. The Council of the North, and the Archbishop and Chapter, met in emergency session and sent for her husband John Foster. Some members of the Council were calling for Anne's body to be contemptuously tipped into the river. John pointed out that he himself was not a recusant, and he could not fairly be blamed for his wife's actions, but "besought their honours to consider that she was but a woman, and being now dead, never could offend them more." The furious Councillors accused him of being a secret Catholic (which he probably was), and continued to abuse Anne, but he replied that "whatever she was, she was his wife, and he bound by the law of God to love honour and protect her, and this being the last and least thing he could do for her, he humbly besought them to give him leave to bury her." It was eventually agreed that he could take her and "put her in her grave", provided it was done without any rites or ceremony. John's resolution of the matter was ingenious: he took her to Holy Cross Church, Pavement, had the grave of Thomas Percy opened, and laid her in it together with the remains of the martyred Earl.

The following January saw Robert Cripling elected as Lord Mayor, despite the fact that his wife never went to church, and he didn't himself if he could help it; he had complained openly about the "railing sermons" preached by the Puritan clergy in York Minster. For the whole of 1579 he ensured that no recusancy fines were collected, but in January 1580 the Council intervened and clapped him in gaol. From that moment on the Corporation came to heel, and gave Lord Huntingdon its full co-operation. In October 1580 all the known recusants in York were summoned to appear before the High Commission, and a great many were terrified into submission, including the Calverts and the Mudds. Margaret was very upset about this, but whichever of the two families had colluded with her over the priest's room did not betray the secret. She herself, though in the early stages of another pregnancy, stood firm and was committed to the Castle for a second period of imprisonment. This time there was no sense of shock; she knew what to expect, and may in a sense have been looking forward to enjoying again that very special sort of community life. It was probably during this second imprisonment that she took up the opportunity to learn to read and write. It meant she could occupy the long hours with spiritual reading, starting with *The Imitation of Christ*.

Alderman Henry May

Theoretically the Council of the North was quite a large body, but its working core was a small group of trained lawyers, paid a regular salary, and obliged to reside permanently in York to be available for government business and preside as judges at court sessions. Lord Huntingdon was careful to nurture his team of professional Councillors, and ensure that the right men were appointed to vacancies: by now all of them were sound Protestants. His growing influence over the York Corporation was exercised in similar fashion, and Henry May continued to do his utmost to demonstrate his ideological correctness, despite the embarrassment of a recusant stepdaughter. When early in 1581 one of York's thirteen aldermen died, creating a vacancy to be filled, the choice fell on Henry May. That same month an Act of Parliament raised the fine for non-attendance at church to a punishing £20 a month. To ensure that children were not given a Catholic education, all schoolteachers now had to be licensed on pain of a year's imprisonment, and a fine of £10 a month for the person employing them.

Margaret was released from prison on 24th April to give birth, and once again John signed a bond, this time of £40, for her good conduct. The bond stipulated that the child be baptised in the parish church within three days of its birth, but when this condition was not met John pleaded poverty (!) and was let off with a fine of 40 shillings. However in August, once again on the Feast of the Assumption, came another raid on Dorothy Vavasour's home, directed by the two sheriffs. Three of the aldermen were also present - one of them being Henry

May. The elderly priest, William Wilkinson, was led through the streets still in his vestments, with two candlesticks carried before him in mockery, and the city riff-raff jeering and spitting. This time Dorothy didn't get away with it: she was imprisoned at the New Counter, one of the Ouse Bridge prisons, with her daughters Anne and Dorothy. So were two of the other laypeople present at the Mass: William Hutton, the erstwhile churchwarden, and his young wife Mary who was pregnant. Although children were never allowed in the Castle, inmates of the Ouse Bridge prisons were able to bring their children to live with them. For the Huttons this was just as well, as they were destined to remain there for a very long time.

Priest martyrs

The Vavasour house was now lost to the Catholic community. Margaret reacted by renting a room at a short distance from her own house in order to set up a second Mass centre. Fr William Hart, one of a flock of brilliant Oxford scholars who had jumped off Queen Elizabeth's gravy train and gone off to study in Douai, was now in York. A very zealous and gifted priest, he used to visit the prisoners in the Castle on a daily basis, bringing both practical assistance and the sacraments. He also served Margaret's Mass centres, and became her spiritual director. Other priests under whose influence Margaret came during this time were Richard Kirkman and Richard Thirkeld.

Previously, the religious offences of Catholics had usually been dealt with by the Ecclesiastical Commission, but the 1581 changes in the law made it possible for Lord Huntingdon to proceed more directly - especially since Councillors, when acting as judges, were not strictly bound by certain provisions of Common Law which might protect the accused. Following a string of high-profile executions of priests in London, he resolved to initiate a tougher line in York. The next two priests to fall into the hands of the Council of the North, in the summer of 1582, were William Lacey and Richard Kirkman. As the law stood it was already possible to sentence a priest to death simply for being a priest, but the government in London had found it too embarrassing actually to do that, and had gone to great lengths to condemn its victims on trumped-up conspiracy charges; most of them had been tortured to try to force them to confess to imaginary plots. Huntingdon's approach was by comparison at least honest and straightforward: Frs Lacey and Kirkman were found guilty of treason on account of their priesthood, and condemned to be hanged, drawn and quartered. On 22nd August they were dragged on hurdles out of the city to the piece of common land known as the Knavesmire, where their attempts to preach to the crowds gathered around the gallows were quickly cut short. A third priest, James Thompson, was executed in November.

In the lead up to Christmas Fr Hart was working so hard that for five nights running he only took two hours sleep. On Christmas Day he said Mass in the house of William and Mary Hutton, which was still available although the family were in prison. That night he fell into bed exhausted, only to be woken by armed men come to arrest him. Imprisoned in one of the Castle dungeons, he was twice brought out for formal disputations with Protestant ministers - once with the Dean of York Minster Matthew Hutton, and another time in the presence of the Council with Bunney and Palmer. As always with such events, the government's version of the proceedings claimed triumph for the doctrines of the state church, while the Catholics circulated a very different story. On 8th March Margaret Clitherow was sent to prison a third time, and so was present in the Castle when Fr Hart was brought back from court under sentence of death. A week later, as he was dragged off for execution, she joined with the other prisoners in calling out to ask for his prayers, and heard him answer calmly, "I will remember each one of you." Before the day ended they had all listened to vivid eyewitness accounts of his heroism in the face of death, from spectators brought to the Castle under arrest for taking relics. Ten days later Fr Richard Thirkeld was arrested, but on the day of his execution the Lord Mayor posted guards on the city gates to prevent people assembling at the Knavesmire. Clearly these executions of priests were not having the impact on the people that they were intended to have.

Fr John Mush

In May 1584 John Clitherow, together with two tradesmen friends, entered into a bond of £100 to obtain Margaret's release for two months. On its expiry in July she returned to prison, but was only kept for a few more months before being once again released under bond. During the summer she had learned, to her joy, of the arrival in York of fresh mission priests to replace those recently martyred. Their activities were co-ordinated by Fr John Mush, a Yorkshireman from a very poor background who had previously been a serving man - possibly in Dr Vavasour's household. Looked down on by some of his confreres for his lowly origins, and for being too plain and blunt in his speech, Mush was highly esteemed by others as intelligent, capable and very brave. Margaret enlisted his help in the arrangements she made later that year to send Henry, her own eldest son who was now about twelve, away to France to become a boarder at the English College in Rheims. John was not involved, for Margaret did not consult him about the decision; he was simply presented with a fait accompli when he returned from one of his trips. Fr Mush's contacts ensured that Henry was placed in the care of a trustworthy courier, probably as one of a small group of

Catholic children being escorted across the Channel. Young boys at the English College were not all seminarians, but he was sure of receiving a good Catholic education there. Margaret did hope he might decide to go on and train for the priesthood.

Margaret had now passed her thirtieth birthday, and her family - both in our sense of the word and the wider one in which she herself would have understood it - had grown quite large. Her stepsons were hulking great lads: William was at university in Oxford, but Thomas wasn't the bookish type and would need to be apprenticed and learn a trade. Those two were almost off her hands, and Henry was safe overseas, but there were plenty of younger children - hers and John's, and always more of other people's being placed with her for their upbringing. In defiance of the new law she now engaged a teacher to run a small school on the premises. This teacher was Brian Stapleton, who had been a prisoner in the Castle when she was last there, and who had since managed to escape. In an attic room which connected with the secret priest's room, he gave lessons to her own children and to two or three others. Of the other children all we know is that one of them is referred to by Fr Mush as "the Flemish boy"; his mother was Dutch, he had been born in the Netherlands and brought to England a year or so previously, and Fr Mush estimated his age as between ten and twelve.

Margaret still managed shop and household as competently and conscientiously as ever, but more and more she dreamed of being able to give it all up one day and become a nun. Lots of busy housewives have dreams of somehow getting away from it all, and often we know that they wouldn't be happy at all if they lost their reasons for being so busy! But in Margaret's case the idea wasn't altogether fanciful. Common sense indicated that she was likely to be widowed while still relatively young; she certainly wouldn't be left penniless, and she could have arranged to slip over the Channel and enter a convent, whereupon her well-established prayer life suggests that she would have settled in well.

When Mass was celebrated in her own house (very early in the morning, before the shop was open) she was always present, devoutly adoring Our Lord made present in the Blessed Sacrament, and receiving Communion twice a week on Wednesdays and Sundays (which for those days was extraordinarily frequent). However when the venue was her other Mass centre - the rented room - she could only attend occasionally: she was too well-known in the neighbourhood, and to be seen going there every day would attract suspicion. Fr Mush found it surprising that she went to so much trouble to ensure that Mass was celebrated when she, personally, could not be there. Even the staunchest of the Catholic laypeople usually confined their risk-taking to ensuring that their own religious needs were met. But Margaret didn't see it that way. Spiritually, if not physically, she was present at Mass each day, and it gladdened her heart to know that the priest would be praying for her while she went about her daily work. But in any case, she explained, "It doth me good and much comforteth me that I know I have you here, and that God is in any way served by my means."

The priest, very conscious of the need for security, felt some misgivings at the freedom with which the schoolchildren were allowed to move around the house. Some of the older ones definitely knew how to get into the secret room, and also about its concealed storecupboard, but apparently not the emergency exit. Possibly, because of the narrowness of the doorway which was easier for them to negotiate than for an adult, they were trusted to fetch things when Margaret was absent. Fr Mush was also alarmed whenever he saw Margaret giving one of her servant maids a sharp telling-off, sometimes with a slap thrown in. What would happen if one of them went off in a huff to the Council? However Margaret considered it her bounden duty to exercise proper discipline. Surely the girls' own parents, who had entrusted them to her, had a right to expect it? As for the maids, who knew that she more often took the dirty work on herself than dumped it on them, they thought the world of her and "had as great a care to conceal her secrets as if they had been her natural children."

The neighbours also loved her, and "would run to her
for help, comfort, and counsel, in their distresses, and how
familiarly she would use them, and with all courtesy and
friendship relieve them." Margaret was saddened to see the
change which only a few years had brought about in public
attitudes: more and more of the local families were losing
their sense of identification with the Catholic faith, and
coming to think of themselves as Protestants. But even the
Protestant ones staunchly guarded her secrets, and made a
point of warning her if they noticed any danger. She still
spoke her mind to them whenever religious and ethical
issues cropped up, and often she didn't have to say very
much before they "would yield to her, and say, 'for God's
sake do what you will, and I am content'." Very few of
them had seriously reworked their inner convictions. They
tended to live on the surface of things and, on that very
shallow level at least, their attitudes were being effectively
and rapidly changed by the psychological pressure of
seeing Protestant positions publicly proclaimed normal and
acceptable, and any open expression of Catholic teaching
derided and punished. So they repeated automatically the
anti-Catholic propaganda they heard around them, without
really thinking what they were saying. Whenever Margaret
was around she could stop that sort of talk "with one word"
and, despite the large number of people living and working
in, or constantly in and out of, her house, she was never
informed on.

Although she had drastically cut down her banquet-going, it didn't mean she and John never enjoyed a night out together. On one occasion when they were both socialising in a neighbour's house, and John had had a few too many, he started having a go at the Catholic faith: "I cannot tell what Catholics are. They will fast, pray, give alms, and punish themselves more than we all, but they are of as evil disposition in other things as we." He then made some really nasty accusations which, since Margaret was the only Catholic present, sounded like a reflection on her personally. Naturally enough, she burst into tears. "Her husband," recounted Fr Mush, "called her 'fool' and said he meant not those words by her, for indeed, he would ever report that he could wish no better wife than she was, except only for two great faults, as he thought, and those were, because she fasted too much, and would not go with him to the church. But all her neighbours, knowing her virtue, comforted her, saying that her husband spake but merrily, and meant no such matter as he said. She answered: 'I pray God forgive him', and no more." Nevertheless she was so upset that she spent most of the night lying awake, turning it over in her mind. By the time she told Fr Mush about it the following day she had got over the personal hurt, and was only sad that John's attitude made it even more unlikely that he would ever become a Catholic himself.

The hanging of Marmaduke Bowes

In March 1585 an Act against Jesuits, Seminary Priests
and other such like disobedient persons made it High
Treason for a priest to be within the Queen's dominions,
and a felony for anyone to "harbour or maintain" a priest.
Sending a child to an overseas seminary would incur a
fine of £100. Shortly after this Act was passed a man who
had often been to Mass at Margaret's house, and
appeared deeply devout, "came to her and in the way and
manner of friendly advice willed her to be more careful
of herself, and since that virtue and the Catholic cause
was now made treason and felony, that either she would
not with such danger receive any priests at all, or else
very seldom; and this he added also, that it was no
wisdom to admit her children and others to God's service,
and that she ought not to adventure upon these things
without licence of her husband." Margaret was hurt and
shocked at his "uncharitable talk". He obviously thought
he was being kind, but her order of priorities was very
different from his. True charity meant firstly to love God
above all things, knowing that only through him could
she, and her family and friends, find true blessedness - if
not in this life, then in the next. So to suggest she should
abandon her own faith, or no longer share it with her
children and her neighbours, was the worst sort of
uncharitableness. Nevertheless, her conversation with this
man did make her wonder whether it was wrong for her

to continue as she was doing without her husband's permission, and she consulted Fr Mush on the point. To her great relief he assured her that she didn't need John's permission to do her duty to God. He also reminded her that it was for her husband's own protection that she must not let him know what she was up to.

Henry May had bought up several adjoining houses to expand his inn, which now fronted on both Davygate and Coney Street. If the ageing Jane was aware that he was sleeping with two of the young women on her staff - Anne Thompson and another girl - she took care not to make a public scandal over it, though according to Fr Mush the whole city knew about it. A poor and unimportant adulterer would have been made to do public penance, but the usual rules didn't apply to aldermen. Jane died in June 1585. In accordance with the terms of her first husband's will, legal ownership of her house - the original nucleus of Henry's now substantial premises - then passed to Margaret. This didn't lead to any immediate upheaval, for complicated divisions of property were often dealt with quite leisuredly and amicably within families, and it seems that Margaret's husband John (who legally controlled her assets) agreed to sell the house to Henry. However before he could actually settle the matter with the Clitherows, Henry would need to build up his capital. His first plan, after a decent interval, was to marry Anne

Thompson, who was of good family and could bring him some additional property.

In September the Earl of Huntingdon instituted yet another crackdown on Catholics. A young schoolmaster was induced under torture first to renounce his faith, and then to betray other people: his information led to the arrest of a priest named Hugh Taylor, and a country squire named Marmaduke Bowes, and in November both were put on trial under the new Act. The judges were four of Huntingdon's most reliable and fiercely Protestant professional Councillors: William Eure who was a Vice-President of the Council, Lawrence Meeres, Ralph Hurlestone, and the Council Secretary Henry Cheke. Taylor was condemned to be hanged, drawn and quartered simply for being a priest in England, but the evidence against Bowes was very confused. Although he seems to have known Fr Taylor well, the priest had not been arrested in his house, and the evidence of the apostate schoolmaster was shown in court to be unreliable. Also, Bowes was not a recusant but a church papist. However the judges were determined to make an example of someone under the recent legislation, *precisely* for the crime of "harbouring", and he was therefore declared guilty. Very often, in such cases, condemned Catholics were offered a free pardon if they would only agree to attend Anglican services, and Bowes wouldn't have had a problem with that at all. But he wasn't given the offer. Realising that there was no escape, he cheerfully accepted as God's will the prospect of being unjustly executed. At some point within the next few days a priest managed to gain access to him in prison, and he was formally reconciled to the Church before being hanged on 27th November.

Trapped in York

Catholics in York took note of the implications: previously it had been just about possible to steer a way through the laws and keep going, but from now on the government might put you to death just for being a Catholic - and you might well find, once in court, that not even apostasy could save you. Margaret, certainly, took note. At every possible opportunity she tried to talk John into giving up the shop and the whole retail side of his business. They could do up the house at Cornbrough and settle down there, and John could concentrate on his wholesale stockdealing. Apart from anything else, it would enhance their social status in the eyes of the world - a prospect which Margaret hoped would attract John, even if it meant nothing to her personally. She couldn't explain to him her real reason for wanting to move out of York. Unfortunately John was the sort of solid and dependable, but unimaginative, husband who feels most comfortable in his role when piling up more and more money, even with no clear plans of what to do with it. He wasn't the least bit interested in becoming a "country gentleman", and on

17th December the lease on the house and shop in the Shambles was renewed for another twenty-one years.

Bowes' martyrdom also worried Henry May. What if Margaret's recusancy and "priest harbouring" landed her in court on the same terms as Bowes? What would it do to his career for the city to see his stepdaughter publicly hanged, and for the Davygate house to be confiscated? On the face of it, Henry now had strong grounds for wanting to protect Margaret and cover up her activities at all costs. But with Huntingdon in charge, the one area of criminal behaviour that influential citizens of York could *not* hope to get away with was the practice and promotion of the Catholic faith. Henry was a clever man, and it occurred to him that rather than trying to safeguard Margaret, he should make sure she *did* get into trouble - just enough trouble to frighten her into giving up all this Catholic nonsense. Meanwhile, the stakes were rising higher than ever: on 15th January 1586, he was elected Lord Mayor of York. On 3rd February he took up his new office, and arranged immediately for a tun of the best Gascony wine to be sent to Lord Huntingdon, at the Corporation's expense. On 15th February he married Anne Thomson.

Margaret's house is raided

On Wednesday 9th March came an order summoning John Clitherow to appear before the Queen's Council. He assumed it was about his son Henry, in the seminary

across the sea, and he had no idea what he was going to
say. Turning up at the King's Manor, which was the
Council headquarters, he found everyone very busy.
Nobody seemed to notice him, so he hung around for a
while and then quietly took himself back home. Next day
came another summons, and this time he was questioned,
but only very briefly before being ordered to come back
straight after dinner. Dinner, which was the first meal of
the day for many people who did not take breakfast, was
eaten shortly before midday, so it was very early in the
afternoon that John returned to the Manor. Soon after he
had left, the two city sheriffs Roland Fawcet and William
Gibson arrived with a band of men to search the house.
They found Margaret busy with her housework. Fr Mush
was in the secret room, together with some people whom
he was instructing, but they were quickly warned and got
away. Brian Stapleton was teaching his school in the attic
when an armed man opened the door, looked in, then shut
it again while he called for reinforcements. Stapleton
went to the door to invite him back in, but then grasped
the situation and slipped out quickly through the priest's
room. The searchers, furious at finding him gone,
searched the house thoroughly from top to bottom,
rummaging through all the storage chests but finding
nothing. They then arrested not only Margaret and the
servants, but also the children. Next they began to
threaten the children. It was the Flemish boy who cracked

first, after the men had taken all his clothes off and threatened him with a beating. He knew the secret of the priest's room, and he showed them where to find the liturgical equipment. This was hard evidence, and was carried off in triumph.

The children and servants were distributed among different prisons around the city, while Margaret was taken straight to the Manor to be interrogated before the four Councillors who had condemned Marmaduke Bowes: Evers, Meeres, Hurlestone and Cheke. What was said during that session is not recorded, but by the end of it Margaret had driven them into a towering rage. They couldn't cope with the fact that she kept smiling cheerfully, and obviously wasn't frightened of anything they could do to her. Perhaps they thought she was too ill-informed to realise how powerful they were. But Margaret wasn't ill-informed. The reason she wasn't frightened was that she was quite certain they were going to kill her. There was no way out of it: she would be put to death within a very short time, and she would die as a martyr, and so go straight to heaven - and so there was no point in worrying.

At 7.00 pm she was brought to the Castle, and placed in a room on her own, apart from the thirty-five other Catholic prisoners, though she could see them in the distance through a window. About an hour later her husband was also brought to the Castle, and sent to a separate room: they were not allowed to speak to each other. The Council left Margaret to stew throughout Friday, and she made good use of the time praying. On Saturday her friend Anne Tesh was brought to join her. Anne found Margaret in such good spirits that from time to time she caught herself, and wondered aloud if it might not be slightly sinful to be so happy under the circumstances. The Councillors, it transpired, had been very busy questioning the Flemish boy, and it was his denunciations that had got Anne arrested. Not long afterwards a messenger arrived to inform Margaret that the child had "accused her for harbouring and maintaining divers priests, but especially two by name, that was, Mr Francis Ingleby of Rheims, and Mr John Mush of Rome. It was reported withal that she should suffer for it according to the new law and statute." The Flemish boy was excellently well-informed, and the government was beginning to build up a plausible case. The news had been announced to Margaret in an attempt to frighten her into a more co-operative frame of mind, but she only laughed and told the messenger, "I would I had some good thing to give you for these good news. Hold, take this fig, for I have nothing better."

On Monday Margaret got dressed and put on her hat, expecting to be summoned before the Assizes, but no summons came, and she and Anne spent the whole morning chatting and joking together. "Sister," said Margaret, "we are so merry together that I fear unless we be parted we shall hazard to lose the merit of our imprisonment." At one point she went to the window, attracted the attention of the Catholic prisoners on the other side of the hall and, laughing, made a sign with her fingers in the shape of a gallows. She was showing them that she knew she was going to die, and wasn't frightened. Dinnertime approached. Margaret recalled that, according to custom, the circuit judges who had come to York to hold the Lent Assizes would be dining at the house of the Lord Mayor, Henry May. Finally, at about 1.00 pm, the gaoler came to tell her it was time to set off for the Common Hall. "God be thanked," she said, "I am ready when you please."

"Margaret Clitherow, how say you?"

At the west end of the Hall sat the two circuit judges, John Clench and Francis Rodes, and with them on the Bench were the four Councillors. Margaret was brought to stand at the bar, and she stood there alone while the indictment against her was read out. Clench then asked: "Margaret Clitherow, how say you? Are you guilty of this indictment, or no?" She stated that she had done nothing wrong. Clench's next question was a standard formality: "How will you be tried?" Margaret was supposed to declare her willingness to be tried "by God and the country". "Country", here, meant a jury. If she would not agree, the trial could not proceed, but the

judges would be obliged to condemn her to death by
"peine forte et dure". It's unlikely that Margaret realised
the implications, but something about the formula rang
an alarm bell with her and she would not repeat it,
insisting, "I will be tried by none but by God and your
own consciences." Accused persons in those days were
not allowed a defence lawyer, and if they got
themselves deeper into trouble through not
understanding the law, that was their tough luck.
However Clench felt sorry for Margaret, and as an
experienced judge he thought she had a good chance of
getting off if the trial went ahead. Although there was
compelling evidence that she had harboured a priest, the
Council had no way of proving that she had done so
since the passing of the statute in March 1585, and
neither of the priests named by the Flemish boy had
actually been taken. Besides, even if she were found
guilty, the court could still exercise clemency so long as
she showed she was sorry and promised not to do it
again. He therefore did his very best to urge her to agree
to be tried. But despite her legal ignorance Margaret
was perhaps more clear-sighted in the matter than the
judge: the fate of Bowes indicated that the Council was
likely to insist that she be found guilty regardless of
legal niceties, and she was determined not to plead for
clemency since she knew that it would only be offered
at the price of public apostasy.

"I believe in God"

Unable to induce her to agree to trial, and hopeing at least to wipe the smile off her face, the judges ordered some confiscated Catholic liturgical equipment to be fetched into court - perhaps the items seized from her own house. A couple of flunkeys were called forward, dressed up in the priests' vestments, and handed chalices. The two started clowning around, putting on a parody of the Mass. They held up unconsecrated hosts, sneering to Margaret, "Behold thy gods in whom thou believedst." Pleased with the little performance, the judges asked her how she liked the vestments. She replied calmly "I like them well, if they were on their backs that know to use them to God's honour as they were made." At this Clench stood up and demanded, "In whom believe you?"

"I believe in God."

"In what God?"

"I believe in God the Father, in God the Son, and God the Holy Ghost; in these Three Persons and One God I fully believe, and that by the passion, death and merits of Christ Jesu I must be saved."

Clench admitted that this was a good answer, and the judges had to try another tack: "Was not your husband privy to your doings in keeping priests?" In answering this question, Margaret's quick thinking enabled her both to avoid directly incriminating herself, and to protect John: "God knoweth I could never yet get my husband in that good case that he were worthy to know or come in place where they were to serve God."

For the time being the court gave up on the situation. Margaret was taken out, and escorted by a large troop of soldiers through the city. She had a supply of small coins with her, and as she walked gave out alms to the beggars on either side of the street, still smiling happily. Her destination this time was the New Counter on Ouse Bridge. That first night her companions were carefully chosen for her: she had to share her "parlour" with a Mr and Mrs Yoward, a couple who were in prison for debt, but known to the authorities as reliably Protestant in religion. However she spent a lot of the evening on her knees praying, and they didn't try to interfere. She also received a visit from Giles Wigginton, Vicar of Sedbergh, who was one of the more eccentric of Lord Huntingdon's Puritan protégés, but when she indicated (rather rudely) that she wasn't interested in listening to his helpful little talk, he left without making a fuss.

No witnesses but children

Next morning at 8.00 am she was back in the Common Hall. Clench tried once again to persuade her to agree to trial, pointing out yet again that there was "but small witness" against her. "Indeed," replied Margaret, "I think you have no witnesses against me but children, which with an apple and a rod you may make to say what you will." When the judges retorted that the items found in her house made it plain that she had priests there, Margaret - without directly admitting the point - argued: "As for good Catholic priests, I know of no cause why I should refuse them as long as I live; they come only to do me good and others." Hurleston, a particularly extreme Puritan, yelled, "They are all traitors, rascals and deceivers of the Queen's subjects." "God forgive you," replied Margaret: "You would not say so of them if you knew them." Eventually Clench brought the discussion back to the main point, whether the prisoner would agree to be tried. She would not. He warned that if she continued to refuse they would be obliged to pass sentence. The Hall was crowded with spectators, and at this point a lot of murmuring arose, in the midst of which Giles Wigginton was shouting to be heard until Clench commanded silence and signalled him to speak out.

"My lord, take heed what you do." besought Wigginton, who was clearly very concerned for Margaret, but had not understood the legal point at issue. "You sit here to do justice; this woman's case is touching death and life - you ought not, either by God's laws or man's to judge her to die upon the slender witness of a boy; nor unless you have two or three sufficient men of very good credit to give evidence against her. Therefore, look to it my lord, this gear goeth sore." Clench stated that he was acting according to the law. "That may well be," cried Wigginton, "but you cannot do it by God's law."

"I thank God heartily for this"

Still Margaret refused to plead. Eventually Rodes burst out, "Why stand we all this day about this naughty, wilful woman? Let us dispatch her." Clench then, as required by law, pronounced the sentence of *peine forte et dure*: "You must return from whence you came, and there, in the lowest part of the prison, be stripped naked, laid down, your back upon the ground, and as much weight laid upon you as you are able to bear, and so to continue three days without meat or drink, except a little barley bread and puddle water, and the third day to be pressed to death, your hands and feet tied to posts, and a sharp stone under your back." Margaret was shocked, not by the death sentence but by the talk about stripping her naked "which methought for womanhood they might have concealed." Nevertheless she replied gently, "If this judgement be according to your own conscience, I pray God send you better judgement before him. I thank God heartily for this." The sheriffs came forward, and this time tied her hands before marching her out of court and back to the prison. With her hands tied it wasn't so easy to hand out money, but she managed as best she could.

From that moment on, access to Margaret was supposed to be strictly controlled, by order of the

Council. But either she managed to evade surveillance,
or else some of her authorised visitors were less
"reliable" than the Councillors thought, for at some point
she had the chance to talk to a friend whom she trusted -
perhaps Dorothy Vavasour, who was also in the New
Counter - and explain why she had refused to be tried.
There were three reasons. The first was that if a trial
went ahead, the only possible witnesses would be her
own children and her wider "family" of schoolboys and
servants: "it would have been more grievous to me than
a thousand deaths if I should have seen any of them
brought forth before me to give evidence against me."
The authorities would certainly be prepared to ill-treat
them as much as was necessary to force them to testify
against her, and probably also to make them embroider
the tale with some nasty lies, to improve the
government's rather weak case. Secondly, it was likely
that some of the more sympathetically pro-Catholic
among her conformist friends and neighbours would be
deliberately included on the jury, not in order to give her
a fair chance, but to put them on the spot to demonstrate
their loyalty to the state religion: "and then they all had
been accessory to my death, and damnably offended
God." There was a third reason which Margaret probably
did state, but which Fr Mush in his account dared not
repeat for fear of incriminating a third party. The secret
room had been constructed not in her house but in her

neighbours' and, if the case came to trial and a proper investigation were made, those neighbours would also be on trial for their lives.

"She is the only woman in the north parts"

Among the authorised visitors were four women neighbours deputed to examine her to establish whether she was pregnant. Predictably, they reported to the Council that they thought she was: in that way they could win her a stay of execution for at least twenty weeks - and a stay of execution would allow more time to campaign for clemency. Lawrence Meeres went with some other Councillors to question Margaret directly on the point, but she answered with strict truthfulness that "she knew not certainly, and would not for all the world take it on her conscience either that she was with child or that she was not." Soon afterwards another group of Councillors, this time led by Ralph Hurlestone and accompanied by some of the Protestant clergy, called on Clench in his room to demand that the execution go ahead regardless of whether Margaret was pregnant. "Mr Hurlestone," answered Clench angrily, "God defend she should die, if she be with child; although she hath offended, yet hath not the child in her womb." Hurlestone insisted he was sure that Margaret was not pregnant, but that in any case: "She is the only woman in the north parts, and if she be suffered to live, there will be more of her order without any fear of law." Clench wasn't happy, but the Assizes were coming to an end and soon he would depart from York. He referred the matter back to the Council. On the day he left he ordered that execution of the sentence be deferred until the following Friday but then "to do as they should think good, if in the meantime they heard not from him to the contrary."

Edmund Bunney and other Protestant divines came to preach at Margaret. Bunney she dealt with by refusing to listen, and reciting professions of faith back at him: "I am fully resolved in all things touching my faith, which I ground on Jesus Christ, and by him I steadfastly believe to be saved, which faith I acknowledge to be the same that he left to his Apostles, and they to their successors from time to time, and is taught in the Catholic Church through all Christendom, and promised to remain with her unto the world's end, and hell-gates shall not prevail against it: and by God's assistance I mean to live and die in the same faith." With Wigginton, who had stood up for her in court, and was so transparently sincere, she was willing to open up a bit. Like other Puritans, he had a thoroughly simplistic understanding of what the Catholic faith was all about, and tried to catechise her on that basis: "How think you, Mrs Clitherow, to be saved?" "Through Jesus Christ his bitter passion and death," promptly replied Margaret. "You say well," acknowledged Wigginton, "but you believe far otherwise, as in images, ceremonies, sacramentals, sacraments, and such like, and not only in Christ." Margaret said firmly, "I believe as the Catholic Church teacheth me, that there be seven sacraments, and in this faith will I both live and die. As for all the ceremonies, I believe they be ordained to God's honour and glory, and the setting forth of his glory and service; as for the images, they be but to represent unto us that there were both good and godly men upon earth, which now are glorious in heaven, and also to stir up our dull minds to more devotion when we behold them; other than thus I believe not." Thrown completely, Wigginton tried lamely to argue that there were only two sacraments, not seven, then gave up. On a second visit he confided in her that he had "seen Christ in a vision", and so was assured of his own salvation. She "began to smile, and made but small answer".

Henry May must have been deeply involved in the preparations for the raid on Margaret's house. It's very likely that he instigated the whole thing - not out of malice, but to forestall something far more damaging. If the authorities really wanted to catch someone like Margaret red-handed, they would have arrived during the morning on a feastday, when almost certainly Mass would be in progress. The very fact that the raid took place on a weekday afternoon in Lent suggests that the whole idea was to find *some* evidence, but not too much. But if the raid *had* been schemed up by Henry in order to give his stepdaughter a nasty fright, to cure her of her

Catholicism, his plans had gone terribly wrong. He visited her in prison and exerted all his famous charm to try to talk her round, but got nowhere, and went back home livid with rage.

"The best wife in all England"

He was not the only one furiously angry with Margaret over her obstinacy. If she had been tried and found guilty, the issues might at least have seemed clearer, but people couldn't understand her refusal to be tried: could it be that she *wanted* to die, and that the whole thing was an elaborate and attention-seeking method of committing suicide? The frustrated anger of a lot of very important men helps to explain the extremely nasty allegations which circulated around York during and after this last week, often originating at the Lord Mayor's dinner table. The authorities sought to exert pressure on Margaret by repeating back some of these slanders. The Flemish boy, they informed her, "had confessed that she had sinned with priests, and that the priests and she would have delicate cheer, when she would set her husband with bread and butter and a red herring. When she heard these words, she smiled and said: 'God forgive you for these forged tales; and if the boy said so, I warrant you he will say as much more for a pound of figs.'" Accusations of adultery she felt able to laugh at. However, even a good marriage relationship is never perfect, and inevitably she had *some* doubts about whether she had always done right by her husband. These could have served her enemies as leverage, but her sound common sense enabled her not to take them seriously: "I trust my husband will not accuse me that I have offended him at any time, unless in such small matters as are commonly incident to man and wife." In fact, those who were trying to blacken her reputation could obtain no support at all from John. When he heard the decision of the court he went berserk, and had a massive nosebleed: "Alas! Will they kill my wife? Let them take all I have and save her, for she is the best wife in all England, and the best Catholic also." Margaret asked to be allowed to speak with him, but was told that to earn that privilege she would have to make some concession - probably by attending an Anglican service, which she was not prepared to do. At the weekend John was released from prison, but commanded by the Council to leave York for five days. He understood only too well why the authorities wanted him out of the way.

Margaret's last night

On Tuesday the Margaret was notified that as soon as the week stipulated by Judge Clench was up, the law would take its course. She "thanked God," but after they had left succumbed to a sense of shock. Soon afterwards she was able to confide to a friend "The sheriffs have told me that I shall die on Friday next; and now I feel the frailty of mine own flesh which trembleth at these news, although my spirit greatly rejoiceth. Therefore for God's sake pray for me and desire all good folks to do the same." But after kneeling down and praying for a while, she declared happily that all her fear had vanished. Over the next three days she observed a total fast, taking neither food nor drink, and spent her time sewing a garment in which to die. She understood that the authorities did not intend literally to drag out the execution over a three-day period as laid down in the sentence, but she was fairly sure she would be obliged to take off her clothes: she hoped to be allowed to put on something else, so long as it was nothing like a normal dress, to preserve minimal decency. It was of plain white linen, very short so as to leave her legs bare, but with long sleeves, and she helpfully sewed lengths of tape to the ends of the sleeves. She arranged for her hat to be sent to her husband "in sign of her loving duty to him as to her head", and for her stockings and shoes to be sent to her eldest daughter Anne, to signify that she should follow in her mother's footsteps by devoting her life to the service of God.

Thursday would be her last night on earth. Margaret was still sharing her room with the Yowards, with whom she was now on friendly terms. She told Mrs Yoward that she was looking forward to her death, but wished she could have the company of one of the Vavasour girls, whose whereabouts within the prison were presumably

less strictly supervised than those of adults. Mrs Yoward
explained that the gaolers had already locked all the
doors, so there was no chance of any of her Catholic
friends being allowed to come and spend the night with
her. Mrs Yoward had been getting ready for bed, but she
dressed herself again and went to kneel beside Margaret.
Shortly before midnight she did go to bed, but only to lie
there dozing fitfully while Margaret remained at prayer.
As the clock struck 12.00 she saw Margaret get up, take
off her clothes and put the linen garment on instead, and
then remain kneeling in the habit until 3.00 am. She then
rose again, went over to the fireside and lay down flat on
the stones for a quarter of an hour. After that she got into
bed and lay quietly until 6.00, when she got up, dressed
and made herself ready. It was Friday 25th March 1586,
the Feast of the Annunciation and, by the reckoning of
the time, New Year's Day. The sheriffs came for her at
8.00, and she greeted them with a smile. She had on her
usual clothes but no shoes or stockings, and they were
shocked to see that her head was bare. A married woman
was supposed always to keep her head covered with a
coif, even indoors, but Margaret had used what was left
of the tape to tie up her hair like that of a bride setting off
for her wedding. Carrying the linen garment over her
arm, she was led out onto the street. It was full of people,
and the execution party had to push its way through the

crowds, but there wasn't far to go: only six or seven yards to the Tollbooth at the end of the bridge.

"I die for the love of my Lord Jesu"

About twenty people assembled in the room, including four women, and some vagrants who had been hired by the sergeants to do the heavy work of the killing. Frost, the Protestant minister in attendance, proposed to Margaret that they should pray together. This was a trick: it would be used as evidence that she had given in at the last minute and joined the state church, so she replied firmly, "I will not pray with you, and you shall not pray with me; neither will I say Amen to your prayers, nor shall you to mine." Frost then urged her to pray for the Queen. Knowing that this, too, was a trick, Margaret knelt down and prayed for the Catholic Church, the Pope, the Cardinals and all the clergy, the for all Christian princes, "and especially for Elizabeth, queen of England that God turn her to the Catholic faith, and that after this mortal life she may receive the blessed joys of heaven." They could hardly say Amen to that. Sheriff Gibson, overcome, stood by the door weeping, leaving his colleague to supervise the execution. Fawcett knew his future prospects depended on doing his very best to stage things according to the government's wishes. Mrs Clitherow," he urged, "you must remember and confess that you die for treason."

"No, no, Master Sheriff, I die for the love of my Lord Jesu."

As she had anticipated, he insisted that she undress completely. Margaret begged that at least the men should turn their backs, and the other women backed her up. They then quickly helped her take her clothes off and put on the linen garment. She lay down on the ground with a handkerchief over her face, a large sharp stone was placed under her back, and a heavy door was laid over her. She put her hands round the door and joined them in prayer, but the sergeants parted them and, using the tapes she had sewn to the sleeves, tied them to two posts so that she lay stretched out in the form of a cross. The officials made a last attempt to get her to pray for the Queen. Margaret said she'd already prayed for her. Finally they suggested that she ask her husband's forgiveness. She replied, "If ever I have offended him, but for my conscience, I ask him forgiveness."

At a sign from the sergeants, the vagrants began piling weights on top of the door. Margaret cried out, "Jesu! Jesu! Jesu! have mercy on me!" and then spoke no more. Witnesses reported that it took her fifteen minutes to die, though she was left there with the weights on top of her for six hours. They were removed at 3.00, and at midnight the sergeants stole out with her body and buried it secretly under a rubbish heap. Fr Mush and her other friends were determined to find it: it took them six weeks, but eventually they found the spot, exhumed Margaret and carried her away on horseback. She was reburied with great reverence a long way from York, but nobody today knows where.

Aftermath

John Clitherow remarried, as Margaret would have expected, and never became a Catholic. However her stepsons William and Thomas held fast to what she had taught them: Thomas went to prison for his faith and died there, whereupon William went to Douai and returned as a priest to serve the English mission. Henry also trained for the priesthood, and apparently decided to join a religious order, but couldn't make up his mind which one; he died in Italy unordained. Anne "followed well in her mother's virtuous steps" as a nun in Louvain.

Margaret Clitherow was canonised in 1970 as one of the Forty Martyrs of England and Wales.

SOURCES

"Memoirs of Missionary Priests" Richard Challoner, revised by J.H. Pollen (Burns Oates & Washbourne, 1924)

"Thomas Percy - Seventh Earl" M.M. Merrick (Duckett, 1949)

"The Puritan Earl: The Life of Henry Hastings Third Earl of Huntingdon" Claire Cross (Macmillan, 1966)

"Margaret Clitherow", Katharine Longley writing as Mary Claridge (Burns & Oates, 1966)

"Catholic Recusancy in the City of York 1558-1791" J.H.C. Aveling (Catholic Record Society, 1970)

"Tudor York", D.M. Palliser (Oxford University Press, 1979)

"Saint Margaret Clitherow", Katharine Longley (Anthony Clarke, 1986)

"The Tudor Housewife" Alison Sim (Sutton Publishing, 1996)

"Food and Feast in Tudor England" Alison Sim (Sutton Publishing, 1997)

"Popular Religion in Sixteenth-Century England" Christopher Marsh (Macmillan, 1998)

"Church Papists" Alexandra Walsham (Boydell & Brewer, 1999)

Informative Catholic Reading

We hope that you have enjoyed reading this booklet.

If you would like to find out more about CTS booklets - we'll send you our free information pack and catalogue.

Please send us your details:

Name ....

Address ....

....

....

Postcode ....

Telephone..

Email ....

Send to: CTS, 40-46 Harleyford Road,
           Vauxhall, London
           SE11 5AY

Tel: 020 7640 0042
Fax: 020 7640 0046
Email: info@cts-online.org.uk  **CTS**